Martial Art Marketing

The No B.S. Guide To Making Money While Building Your Brand

By
Aaron J. Perry

© 2013 by Aaron J. Perry

ISBN-13: 978-1493683819

ISBN-10: 1493683810

All Rights Reserved. No part of this publication may be reproduced in any form or by any means, including scanning, photocopying, or otherwise without prior written permission of the copyright holder. Reviewers may quote brief passages in reviews

First Printing, 2013

Printed in the United States of America

Liability Disclaimer

By reading this book, you assume all risks associated with using the advice given below, with a full understanding that you, solely, are responsible for anything that may occur as a result of putting this information into action in any way, and regardless of your interpretation of the advice.

You further agree that our company cannot be held responsible in any way for your success or failure as a result of the information presented in this book. It is your responsibility to conduct your own due diligence if you intend to apply any of this information in any way

No part of this publication may be reproduced or transmitted in any form or by any means, mechanical or electronic, including photocopying or recordings, or by any information storage and retrieval system, or transmitted by emailwithout permission in writing from the author.

Adherence to all applicable laws and regulations, including international, federal, state and local governing professional licensing, business practices, advertising and all other aspects of doing businessin the US, Canada, or any other jurisdiction is the sole responsibility of the purchaser or reader

Neither the author nor the publisher assumes any responsibility or liability whatsoever on the behalf of the purchaser or reader of these materials.

Any perceived slight of any individual or organization is purely unintentional.

I sometimes use affiliate links in the content. This means if you decide to make a purchase, I will get a sales commission. But that doesn't mean my opinion is for sale. Any affiliate links contained in this material are for products and services that I have personally used and found useful. Please do your own research before making any purchase online.

Terms of Use

You are given a non-transferable, "personal use" license to this book. You cannot distribute it or share it with other individuals.

No part of this publication may be reproduced or transmitted in any form or by any means, mechanical or electronic, including photocopying or recordings, or by any information storage and retrieval system, or transmitted by emailwithout permission in writing from the author.

Also, there are no resale rights or private label rights granted when purchasing this book. In other words, it's for your own personal use only.

About The Author

Aaron J. Perry (AJ) is a native of Auckland, New Zealand but currently lives in Brisbane, Australia.

AJ started his Martial Arts journey in 1990 and has trained in Zen Do Kai and American Kenpo.

AJ began his publishing career as the author of **"Martial Games for Kids"**, an Instructors manual for making Martial Arts Lessons more enjoyable and productive for students and teachers. The Martial Games also resulted in attracting new students and longer retention of existing students for Martial Arts Schools all around the world in a wdie variety of martial arts styles

The success of his first book lead to the Monthly **Martial Games Newsletter** for Instructors, it provides online and offline marketing methods along with new Martial Games and Instructor Insights to keep Instructors motivated and always moving forward with their business growth and their teaching methods.

Visit **www.martialgames4kids.com** for more details about the Martial Games Manuals and the highly respected Monthly Newsletter Membership.

As the Chairman of **Martial Art Marketing** he has helped hundreds of Martial Arts School

Owners grow their student numbers and increase their profits using step by step techniques to develop their school as the Authority in their local area.

AJ Perry is also a founding member and registered MMA Australasia Official. He can often be found cageside as an official Judge at Australian MMA Events.

For more information about AJ Perry's Martial Arts Information Products and Services please visit the following official websites.

AJ's Official Websites:
http://www.martialgames4kids.com
http://www.martialartmarketing.com
http://www.aaronjperry.com

Table of Contents

About The Author 6
Results In Advance 10
Why Build A Brand? 13
How To Design Your Logo/Brand 15
Make Your Students Feel Like Family 17
   How to Design your T-shirt... 19
Quick n' Easy Profits With Teespring Tees 23
Brand All Your Gear 31
How To Really Drive Your Message Home 33
The Humble Old Bumper Sticker 39
Don't Be Shy With Your Signage 43
Don't Forget About Your Own Home Base 45
   Review Your Room... 49
Quick Image Guide For Branding Online 51
Attractive Vs Powerful Business Cards 53
Your Branding Tracker Checklist 59
Thank You 61
Acknowledgements 63
Resources 65
   Royalty Free Images 65
   Graphic Designers 65
   Tees and More 65

Results In Advance

We live in an age where there is Information Overload. There is no shortage of information but there is a shortage of useful, practical, high quality information.

It can be difficult finding the diamonds in the rough because no one has enough spare time to read through all the crap that is available and besides you don't want to waste your time learning and using information that doesn't work.

Bad information could even send you in the wrong direction costing you time, money and future business.

This is why I believe in providing you with RESULTS IN ADVANCE.

The Martial Art Marketing series of books contain Marketing Information used successfully by Martial Arts Schools around the world to grow their businesses. It is a collection of some of the best marketing advice I have shared with my Inner Circle Members over the past decade.

This information has helped hundreds of Martial Arts Schools attract new students, retain existing students and add additional profit streams so that they can grow and have fun while doing it.

Why did I write this book?

I wrote this book for you. I've deliberately released this great information at the lowest price possible so you had no sensible reason to not get this book.

I've also written it because it's my way of offering you...

"RESULTS IN ADVANCE"

Read through this book chapter by chapter and take action on each of the Marketing techniques. You don't have to speed through it in a week, take your time to get one thing working before moving on to the next but always keep moving forward. If you get stuck on something then move on to the next chapter. Continually keep building on your marketing and branding.

The information in here can have great results for you but it all comes down to you taking action on the information provided. Sadly this means that legally I can't make any guarantees for your personal results but there is nothing in these pages that hasn't benefitted my Inner Circle Members.

If I can help you add just one new student into your Martial Arts School then it's already paid for the price of this book. That one extra student's training fees can also more than cover the cost of becoming an Inner Circle Member.

But I don't want you to add just one new student. I want to help you attract so many new students that you have to start a waiting list.

I also want to help you retain your current students because the most rewarding thing as an instructor is seeing your students progress through to Black Belt and beyond for many years, because learning a martial Art isn't a short course, it should be a lifelong journey and enjoyed every step of the way.

I know the power of the info inside this book and what it could do for you and your martial Arts School so PLEASE don't let it sit on your bookshelf and collect dust or get lost amongst the digital downloads on your tablet.

Make the most of this opportunity and the Results will speak for themselves.

When you get those Positive Results then you'll know you can trust me and you can confidently move forward with more of my Martial Art Marketing Information.

I look forward to hearing your success stories.

Why Build A Brand?

A lot of Instructors want to build their own Martial Art School, but only a few build a Brand.

Branding is something that fashion labels and soft drink companies do. Nike, Armani, Coke and Pepsi are all Brands. They are businesses that have a product that people buy because they know and for some reason trust.

A Brand is simply a business name or logo that has become recognised as a leader in it's field. The big companies spend a fortune on advertising to achieve and maintain that recognition in the general community. Nike started out making shoes but now they also make apparel and regular people pay good money to buy their t-shirts and shorts a wear them proudly (They are paying Nike to help advertise their brand, these people are called Fans)

I am going to show you some great ways to start building your Martial Art School as a Brand. I understand that you don't have money to burn and personally I think paying for expensive ads, billboards, radio spots etc are a poor investment in your future.

I'll Show You How To Advertise AND Make A Profit At The Same Time...

People always assume that advertising will cost them a lot of money and if you only know the standard ways then you're right. But there are ways to get your name out there in very targeted ways at no cost.

I've always maintained that making your students raving fans of your business is the best and cheapest way to attract more students. Now I'll show you three ways to take advantage of your best asset... **Your Current Students!**

The Guys, Girls and Kids that train with you already know you are a talented Instructor and will happily promote you to prospective students. Your aim over the next few months is to grow the exposure of your school to the general public through your current students and smart Brand placement.

It always sounds better when someone else speaks your praises rather than self promotion.

I hope you take on board all of the info in this book and take action to get it happening ASAP because I will have more for you to work on in following books from the Martial Art Marketing series.

Read these marketing ideas and make them happen. You can make more money and your Martial Art School can really be getting noticed.

How To Design Your Logo/Brand

You probably already have a Logo for your Martial Arts School and may not need to do anything but please don't skip reading this short chapter...

Branding is about making your Logo recognizable, building a meaning behind the logo so that it is a symbol of what you do, who you are, what you're all about.

This might sound all arty farty but it's common sense refined into simple design.

Imagine a bad example to start with...

If you own a Kickboxing Gym and want to attract young kids to sign up and start training with you then having a logo of a Bloody Axe is not going to encourage most parents to enter your door and enroll their precious child.

Likewise if you have a logo that shows a cute kid in thai shorts and gloves then you may struggle to attract adults that want to compete at a high level.

Think about your perfect student. Do you want to fill your classes with friendly kids, competitive kids, casual adults or hardcore adults?

Your Logo should resemble your ideal student demographic. A simple image can tell a lot about you and your Martial Arts School so make sure it is saying what you want it to say and to the right people.

This book focuses on using your Logo to Brand your business. This involves t-shirts, caps, uniforms, stickers, flyers, posters, internal and external signage, emails, etc

I want you to make sure that you have a Logo you are proud of before continuing any further.

Once you start building your brand you don't want to make changes. Look at brands like Coke, Nike, Sony... they have spent millions (possibly billions) on their logos and they never change them.

I've worked with Sony, Pizza Hut and KFC and they have incredibly tight guidelines on how their brand/Logo is displayed. All three are very succesful companies and the only one that made a change in the past 50+ years was Kentucky Fried Chicken swapping to KFC because of all the bad press about unhealthy fried food.

If you're not sure about your current logo or want to see some options then I suggest posting a design job on http://99designs.com explaining who your ideal customer/student is and see what everyone comes up with. Set a limit on the price you are willing to pay for the winning design.

For a cheaper option you can find some great royalty free images at http://www.123rf.com which can be used to create a new logo.

If you have creative students in your class then you may be able to enlist their help and get the design done for free. They will be proud to see their design work used to represent their Martial Arts School.

Make Your Students Feel Like Family

I believe every Martial Art School needs to have its own Club Uniforms and most do.

Your students probably wear a Karate Uniform in white or black with a coloured belt when they train with you. Modern MMA schools don't wear the traditional Gi and opt for MMA shorts and T-shirt or Rash Guards.

Whatever your students wear when training, it should have your school name and logo on it, maybe even a slogan.

A Club Uniform has many advantages...

1. It makes your students feel like part of the club, a team... A Family Member!
2. It sets a standard for dress when training
3. It can earn you extra profit for your school
4. <u>It can be seen by outsiders (the general public)</u>

Point 4 is the one that interests me most for marketing. If your students are seen wearing your schools name then they are helping you advertise your school and not only is it free for you but you can actually make a small profit when selling them that uniform.

A training uniform is normally only going to be seen inside your school or briefly in the car park as your students come and go from the venue, or at competitions, demos and seminars. This is all good but you are missing out on the bigger audience which is the general public.

I admit that I do see kids wearing their training Gi while shopping with their parents before or after their lessons but that's just it. They don't wear that Gi in public on days that they're not training.

Now I don't think your students should be going out in their normal life doing everyday things wearing a Martial Art Gi. I have seen one 20yo guy doing his grocery shopping in his gear and personally I thought he looked like an idiot... the first time I just assumed he needed to do it and had no choice but I have seen him a number of times, shopping, getting his hair cut, I think the guy is just a nutter that want everyone to think he's a lethal weapon.

What I do recommend for every Martial Arts School is a selection of casual clothes that your students can wear as normal clothing... t-shirts, caps and hoodies are the best. These items can be worn all the time and they are easily seen/noticed by people, especially if you make them look good. You should already have your MA Schools name, font and logo so your design is half done. If you want to you can do the layout and design yourself or you can find a screen-printer and they will have someone that can work with you. If you're lucky you can probably get one of your students to help you out which will be much cheaper (or free).

How to Design your T-shirt...

1. Make sure that the School name is in a large easy to read font on the front and back.
2. Put your suburb location/s under the name in a small font
3. Add your Logo or Slogan on front (smaller) and back (larger)
4. If you have a website, put it on the back near the bottom in clear large font…
(Don't worry about keeping the www at the start, everyone knows it's a website when they see the .com at the end)

I suggest you keep the front of the t-shirt design smaller as some students won't want to feel like they are wearing a billboard. Also most people will be able to read the details when they are talking to the student, they will be close so it can be smaller and still work....

On the back however I suggest you go **BIG**. This should be recognizable and readable from a distance so anyone walking/standing behind your student can see the school name, slogan and website address.

How Much Will This Cost?

The answer to this is why I love designing clothing for students. Yes it will cost money to get the gear made but you will sell it to your students, friends and the parents of your students and make a profit. You can make extra cash to go towards new training gear while having your students proudly promoting your MA School outside of training.

You Can Collect Money Before Printing...

The other benefit of already knowing who your customers are... you can pre-sell the clothing before placing your order with the screen-printers. Work out the designs, colours, sizes and items and then give an order form to your students and give them a week (or two) to select which items they would like to order. Get them to pay for their selection when they return the order form.

By doing this you will have the money up front to pay the screen-printer and you will know exactly the colours, sizes and quantities that you need to order. With the extra money you have made as profit I recommend you order some extra quantities of the most popular sized items which you can continue selling to new and current students.

When the gear arrives and you start handing it out to your students they will see what everyone else got and no doubt you will get some students wanting more items straight away. Your proud student can now wear your branded gear everywhere... to the movies, out shopping, playing in the park, when they go jogging or walking the dog, etc...

I'll tell you right now it puts a huge smile on your face when you are out doing something and you see someone wearing one of your t-shirts or caps while hanging out with their friends.

Believe me, your students will soon come up to you and tell you stories about strangers approaching them to ask about the t-shirt and where they train and what it's like.

There is no better endorsement for your school than a proud student saying good things on your behalf.

One company has started printing t-shirts using the crowd funding business model. This means you can design your t-shirt on their website, set the minimum quantity required to be purchased before they are produced and you can set the price you want.

This means you have no up-front costs to cover and when enough t-shirts are ordered the company will print and ship them for you and then deposit the profit made directly to your Paypal account.

You do have a limited time span for your design to be purchased so make sure you inform your students when they will be available for ordering.

I'll explain this option in more detail in the next chapter.

Quick n' Easy Profits With Teespring Tees

Teespring makes it very easy for you to design and sell t-shirts without spending any of your own money.

Go to www.teespring.com and follow along...

Take a moment to watch the short video explaining teespring then click on the **Get Started** button...

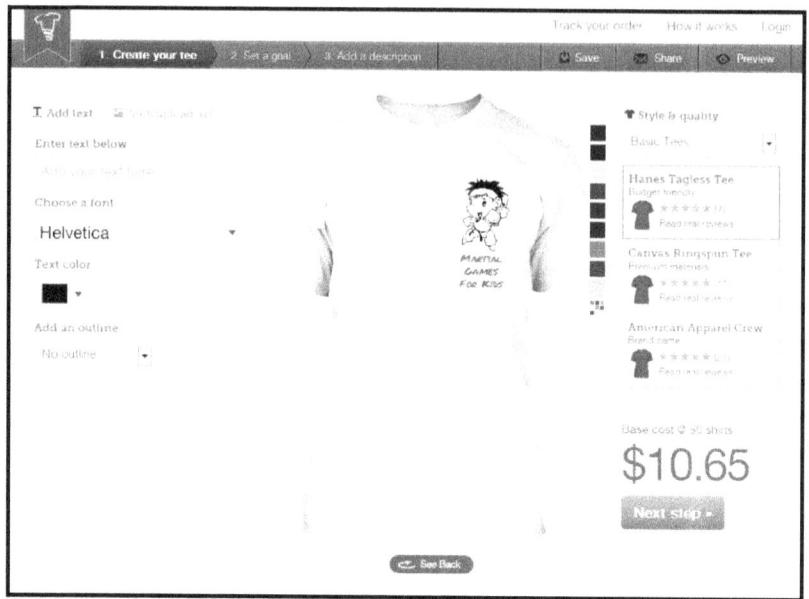

On this screen you can add your text and pictures to the front and back of the t-shirt.

Take some time to experiment with the text font, size and color until you are happy.

Remember each color you add to the design will increase the production cost for printing so find a balance between eye-catching design and profitable design. The website automatically adjusts as you change the design to show you the printing cost (based on 50 tees)

For the Graphics you should already have your Logo designed to add onto your t-shirt but if you want to add additional images to the Front or Back Teespring has a royalty free library of images you can use.

You can also get good quality images from 123rf.com for around $6-$10 each.

I suggest making your image on the back of the t-shirt as large as possible so it can easily be recognized at a distance. This is your Branding, when people see this image they should know it represents your Martial Arts School.

Teespring allows you to have differnt colored tees and different quality tees, play around with your options on the right hand side of this page and keep an eye on the estimated printing cost to ensure you don't get too high.

This is a custom t-shirt for your students so you can charge a little more than average but ideally keep them reasonable.

You want to make a profit from this but remember the main goal is getting the tees onto your students so they wear them out in public because that is high quality free advertising for you and your business.

When you are happy with your design move on to the next step which is setting the selling price of your t-shirt and the minimum order threshold that has to be reached for them to be printed.

For this example I've set the sale price at $19.95...

Here you can see the difference that the minimum quantity makes on the profits... for 20 tees the profit is $5.99ea... for 50 tees the profit is $9.30ea

Set your minimum quantity relative to the number of students you have. If you aim too high and you don't reach the minimum then no tees will be printed and you make nothing... If you're close then buy the extras to get it over the tipping point. You can always sell them later to new students.

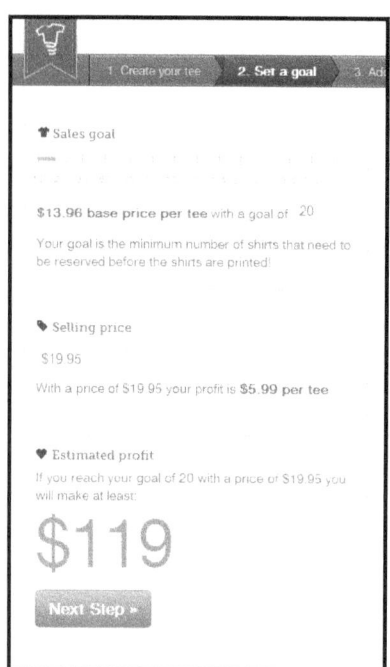
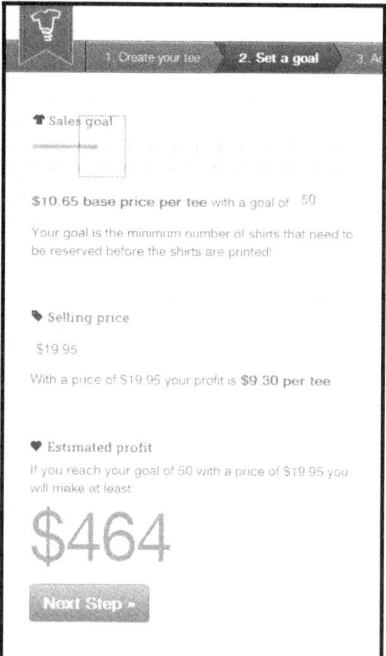

Now that you have set your minimum order quantity and the price you can move on to the final step which is adding a Title and Descrition for the Sales Page.

Set the length of the campaign, generally I find 14 days is best, it gives you time to promote it but also gives them a short time frame to take action before it disapears.

Also set the URL link for the Sales Page... It's best to name this after your school if possible so it's easy for your students to remember it and they know it is specifically for them (not just some random t-shirt you are suggesting they buy)

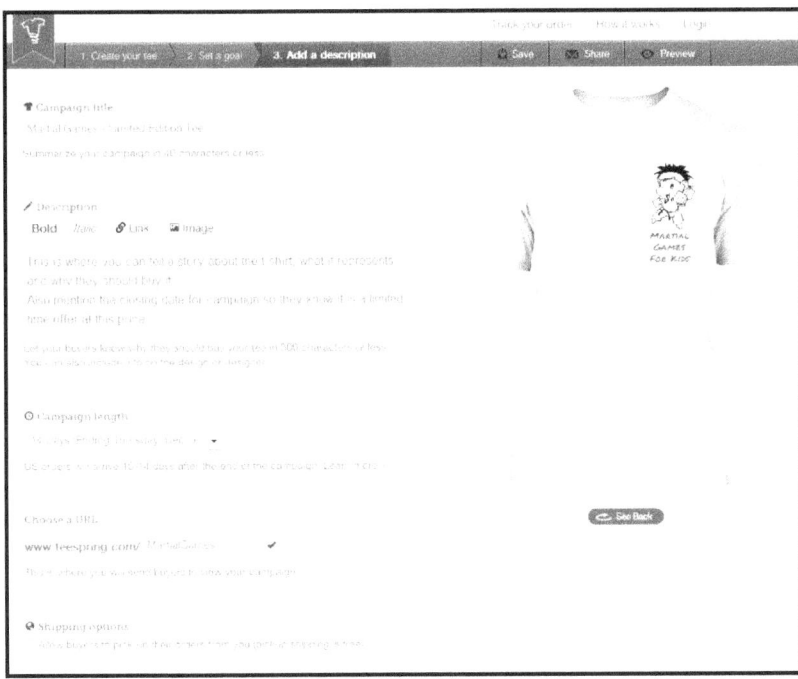

Click on **Preview** to see what your Sales Page will look like. This is where you will send your students to purchase the Tees.

Don't click on **Launch Your Campaign** until the day you start promoting it to your students.

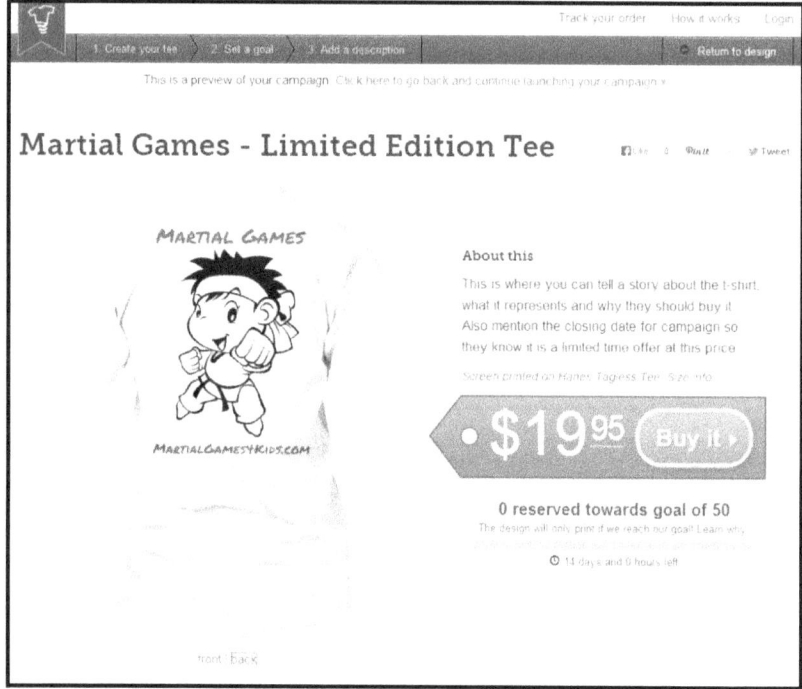

Remember the clock starts counting down as soon as you launch the campaign so get all your promo material (email with links, A4 or A5 rpintout to give to students/parents during the lesson) ready before launching,

Note: On this Sales Page you can also offer the students to the option to select collecting their order from you to save on shipping costs.

To maximise your profits you want higher volume orders of any design you choose but you could do new designs a couple of times a year if you have a large student base.

Keep your main Logo/Brand image consistant so that it continues to build it's recognition in the greater community.

You can still have fun adding new slogans or adding additional graphics around your main Brand Image.

Look at other successful brands for inspiration on how to use a single brand image in many creative ways eg. RedBull, T&C Surf, TapOut, Nike, etc

Another great option is having a design contest amongst your students. Let them come up with fresh designs that they want to wear. Select the designs that best promote your Martial Arts School and then get the students and parents to have the final vote on which design will be printed.

This is great way of getting everyone involved and creating some buzz for the new t-shirts beofre you get onto Teespring and launch your campaign.

I suggest a Main T-shirt for all students to begin with, then follow up later with seasonal t-shirts/hoodies/long sleeve t-shirts.

You can have a kids design and a seprate Adults design if you have enough students in each.

You can also create new designs for adults and kids each year

It won't make you a fortune selling t-shirts but it provides excellent exposure of your brand out in the world.

Brand All Your Gear

The possibilities are almost endless with todays printing companies.

You can have your Brand placed on Gym Bags, Pens, Coffe Cups, Mouse Pads, etc

If you want to make money with these products then find a printer and place an order then put the products in your Pro Shop for students to buy. This is more profitable but it requires you spending money upfront and waiting for sales.

Another option is using a Print On Demand company like CafePress. You simply upload your design and select the items you want to be available for your students to buy. Now they can order the items online and you make a small profit for every item sold. www.cafepress.com

The most popular products with students are T-shirts, Gym Bags and Hats. Every student should have a gym bag so these are worth sourcing and selling as part of every new students sign-up along with their uniform.

How To Really Drive Your Message Home

Outdoor Advertising is a Great way to attract New People that may have never heard of you because they are outside your normal circles of impact.

Billboards can give you great exposure but they cost a lot to set up and your time is limited. You will be billed every month or they will give your spot to someone else… but there is another option and it's sitting in your driveway right now.

Vehicle Advertising is surprising cheap to set up and once it's paid for it's done and you can reap the benefits of getting your message out in public for years.

If you own your own vehicle you can go all out and get large graphic signage done on all sides.

If you can't put on permanent vinyl wrap graphics for some reason (company car, borrowed car, shared car) then you can get magnetic signs made so that you can put them on when you drive around and then remove them quickly when you need to.

Basic Guidelines for Signage:

· **Use Clear Font** (easy to read)
· Have Contact Phone Numbers
· **Have Website URL**
· Have Email Address

Extra Guidelines for Signage:

· **Have a Special Offer** (Gift or Discount)
· Have Gift/Discount Code Word
· **Brief Description of Your Services**

Always make sure your vehicle is kept clean and tidy and you can no longer have fits of road rage - blasting your horn, flipping off other drivers, etc. When your vehicles are well signed you are on display to the world and have to maintain a good image to promote your school.

You may even want to get a new/old car that suits the image of your school. Something that captures attention more than average.

Red Bull have racing mini's and convertible VW cars to get noticed. An exterminator has an old hearse with a dead bug on top. A local home computer repair guy has an ambulance and my friend with the MMA Gym owns a H3 Hummer.

I gave him a hard time about buying the Hummer because it was soooo stereotypical but that's exactly why he got it. The young guys at his gym love it and they love going to fight shows in it. MMA Event organizers let him park right near the front doors because it's good advertising for both of them.

Here's a short funny story...

A couple of months ago he stooped at a shopping centre to get some groceries and when he returned to the carpark he found his Hummer almost in the next parking space because someone had run into it so hard and smashed up the front corner.

While he was standing around waiting for the tow truck to come and collect his poor smashed baby an old man drove in, parked his car and hesitantly walked up to him...

The old guy apologized and explained that his young daughter had come to the shops and when she didn't see the Hummer when she was backing out (She Must Be Blind) and when she saw it she quickly jumped on the accelerator instead of the brake and hence smashed into it at speed.

She got out to look at the damage and then saw the signage on the side of the Hummer. When she realized it was owned by an MMA Gym/Fighter she panicked and drove away because she was scared about what would happen to her.

When she got home still shaking, she told her dad what had happened and thankfully he came back to the scene to meet the Hummer's Owner and give him their insurance details.

This brings up another point... Always park your vehicle where it will get noticed. Try to park it on busy streets or near other places that have the same types of customers as your school.

If your ideal students are kids then you can park your car near school grounds, play grounds, family parks, sporting fields, amusement parks, etc. Thankfully you won't be considered a creepy stalker when parking outside these places because all your contact details are displayed on the outside of your vehicle. But it's still a good idea to park your car and then leave it as it does look strange if you just sit in it watching kids all day.

You can also leverage vehicle advertising with your students...

Other options...

- **Bumper Stickers**
- Rear Window Decals
- **Spare Tire Covers** (on 4x4s)
- Magnetic Signs
- **License Plate Covers**

You can get any or all of these things custom printed to advertise your school and give them or sell them to your students to put on their cars, vans, SUVs.

This could give you an extra 30, 50, maybe 100 extra vehicles on the road advertising your school every day of the year.

If that generates 1 or 2 extra phone enquiries each week that's a great result for a low cost marketing method.

Another bonus is that the parents with the your Ad on their car can also be your best advocate when questioned by curious people that ask them about your school and what it's like.

Their support of your school speaks highly of how good you must be for them to display it in public and proudly be associated with you.

The prospective students that come from this kind of first contact are already preconditioned to think that you will be great and that they will like you, just like the family they met and talked to.

Get Your Message On The Road!

The Humble Old Bumper Sticker

I'm old enough to remember when bumper stickers were a massive craze.

Every petrol station had a rotating stand with a selection of bumper stickers to choose from. The simple 2 colour ones and the crazy rainbow reflective ones. Nearly everyone had their own design, from radio stations and rock bands to environmental groups, local stores and high schools.

They still exist but not like they used to. Bumper stickers are however still a cost effective way of getting your MA School noticed. The cost of getting a couple of hundred stickers made is actually quite cheap and you can either sell them to your students or give them away.

I suggest selling them for more than they cost but keep the price under $2. I have found that if you give something for free it often gets lost but if you sell it to them for a couple of bucks they will go and put it on their car, bike or skate board straightaway. People appreciate things that they have paid for much more than something they receive for free.

Bumper stickers were a great fun craze and as I mentioned a lot of stores had stands made specifically to hold all the choices (just like a postcard display stand you may see when on holiday). This meant that all the stickers were the same size and that is why we know them as bumper stickers.

Don't restrict yourself to the standard bumper sticker dimensions. People these days are happy to put stickers on their back windows or the tailgate of their truck or the back door of their 4x4 or SUV so you can get the sticker made in almost any size and shape you want. It is best to find a supplier and discuss the prices and options before getting too set on the design. Remember that you want a cool looking sticker but you don't want to make it too expensive for you or your students.

What Should It Say

Keep it simple as it will most likely be on the back of a car so the reader will probably be in a car sitting behind them at the traffic lights. Look at your sticker the same as a business card. It should have your MA School name, your Logo and possibly a Slogan and definitely your website address if you have one (which you really should)

Don't try to fit too much on it as the more you squeeze on, the smaller the text has to be. You want the school name and website address to be clearly visible from a distance. Also use a clear, easy to read font. DON'T get too clever and fancy with the design... if people can't read it or understand it then it is a complete waste of space.

For this type of advertising simplicity is King

If you can't take in all the information off the sticker in less than 5 seconds then it is probably too complicated and it won't get read or remembered...

What's The Point?

You are achieving two goals here...

1. You are getting your Students to become proud fans of your business and help you advertise it without it actually costing you anything.

2. You are turning your MA School into a well recognized Business/Brand in your local community.

Over the next couple of months you should have most of your students driving around with a sticker on their car and a t-shirt on their back or a cap on their head. Your Martial Arts Schools Name and Logo (Brand Image) will be seen by thousands of people and your Brand will be recognized as a part of you and your school.

Note: Some people don't want to be a local celebrity.

I don't want to be famous like an Actor because

then you have no privacy but it is great when people in your industry recognize you and respect what you do. For any business to be a success it has to be out in the open, seen and recognized. When someone in your area thinks about learning Martial Arts they should automatically think about contacting you. They should know that you are a professional MA School with proud students.

If they are new to the area and they ask anyone where to train you should be the first place everyone recommends.

All of the small things like Stickers, T-shirts, Caps, a Website, PDF Brochures, Business Cards all add up exponentially increasing your schools profile in your local community.

Don't Be Shy With Your Signage

This is one of the most obvious places to advertise and you should always make the most of it.

External Signage has two main functions:
1. It tells strangers what you do and where you are
2. It tells prospective students where you are

There is nothing worse than talking on the phone to a new potential student, arranging a meeting and then not having them show up because they couldn't find your building.

The size and style of your signage will be controlled by the venue you use.

If you use a rented location part time then you may not be able to do too much in the way of permanent signage but you can still place Pop-Up Banners or Sandwich Signs outside the venue while you are training so the people passing by will see them.

If you have a permanent space then you can add graphics to the outside of your building on the windows (eye level) to be seen by people walking past, also on the top of the building to be seen from a greater distance.

Walk outside of your building and look at which direction people can see your building, it could be from an adjacent road, on a main road, near a school bus stop, etc. Aim your signage to be seen easily by the most people.

If you have a lot of traffic driving by at night invest in lit signage so that it stands out and is noticed. Unlit signage only works half of every day

Make sure your Logo/Brand Image is large and easily seen. The effect of branding is cumulative and as people start seeing your brand on t-shirts, bags, caps, your car it will sink into their mind, then when they see the signage on your building they will think **Oh, so that's where everyone around here trains Martial Arts.**

If they decide they want to learn a Martial Art then they already know where you are. If someone mentions that they want to learn a Martial Art they can tell them about this place they know that they drive past all the time.

Don't Forget About Your Own Home Base

Not All Signage Has To Be Outside!

When most people think about signage they think about the signs on a building, the sign above the door, billboard signs, maybe posters up in public. Internal Signage is almost never acknowledged.

Internal Signage is material seen by people once they have entered into your school. If you have a permanent venue then you have to take full advantage of this opportunity.

Place a Large Image of your Logo on a wall (or all walls) that is clearly seen. The bottom of the logo image should be 7ft (2 metres) from the floor. This allows you to take group photos at gradings, seminars, Christmas Parties, etc with your Logo as the background.

This is a great social feature now with the help of Facebook, Twitter, Instagram, etc where you can post these photos and tag all of the people in the photo so that it appears on their page for their friends and family to see. All of these photos that get shared around, liked and commented on have your Martial Arts School Logo working like a billboard in the background. This kind of social marketing is subtle, natural and priceless. It gives you great value and social proof while costing you absolutely nothing once the signage is up on the wall.

You can get many years of free viral marketing by placing your Internal Signage in the right place so that proud students and parents sharing their photos are happily advertising your school for you.

If you're teaching at a part time venue you can still get some large pop up banners for a couple of hundred dollars which can be placed on each side for group photos.

Students and parent love showing off photos of successful gradings or a photo of a seminar they have attended. Make the most of every opportunity.

Along with your Branding make sure you continue marketing and informing your students. Even if you teach at a shared or rented location you can still do some of the following to boost your image/reputation and educate all that enter about what you can do for them.

Show Off Your Services...
If you have an entry/waiting area then supply informational brochures about all of the services you provide. Make brochures for each type of class that you teach eg. Kids Classes, Adult Classes, Women's Classes, Fitness Classes, Stretching Classes, Anti-Bullying Classes, etc

If you have classes or seminars for particular groups or for certain skills then make a brochure/flyer and a poster for every one of them and get them on display where everyone that enters your school will see them.

If you're not already doing this then you will be surprised by the number of people commenting that they never realized you ran these classes. They are so focused on just getting the kids in and out on time that they have never noticed that there are classes that may interest them.

Boost Your Credibility...
Rather than fill the waiting area with old magazines to read, put in useful reading material of your own.

Have a folder filled with the Glowing Testimonials you received a couple of months ago for new visitors to look through. This will give them an insight into why they should stick with you and gives them more confidence that they chose wisely to bring their kids into your school because other parents have written great things about you.

Provide Constant Updates...
You can make a simple newsletter that keeps everyone up to date on upcoming events, special promotions, class times, success stories and add in some quick testimonials.

This type of newsletter doesn't have to be a daunting task to make. Only a small portion has to be specific to your school. The rest can be filled with related news, puzzle games, inspirational quotes, jokes for kids.

You can even ad in some small ads for other local businesses in exchange for them promoting your school to their customers.

Acknowledge Your Success...
If you have been featured in an article then blow it up and display it on a wall (also add it into the Testimonial Folder).

Also display your certificates and any awards and or trophies you may have won. Don't be shy about your accomplishments.

Acknowledge Others Success...
Likewise display articles, trophies, awards that your students have received whenever possible.

Everyone likes to be acknowledged and showing that your students are having successful lives inside and outside the dojo will also make you look good as part of their circle of influence.

I love seeing Instructors publically acknowledge their students successes on Facebook and Twitter as well as inside their school. Not just for Martial Arts related success but also for other achievement like becoming school captain, great exam results, making it to finals in another sport, for doing volunteer work, etc.

Review Your Room...

As a New Person...
Enter your training space and look at it objectively as if you were a new potential student (or parent) and look at what's on display.

What does it say about you and your school?

What can be added to help a new person find out more about who you are and what your school can offer them?

· Can you see when training times are?
· What Classes are Available?
· What Qualifications do you have?
· Do You Appear Successful?
· Do You Appear Friendly/Well Liked?
· What are Your Students like?

All of these questions will go through the mind s of new visitors. Some questions will be more important than others but your internal signage should supply favorable answers to all of these questions for new visitors.

As a Current Student...
Enter your training space and look at it as if you are a current student or the parent of a young student and ask yourself those same questions.

Maximize Your Internal Signage

Make the most of all these opportunities inside your very own four walls.

It costs very little time and money to add great information inside your school and it's all up to you. There are no restrictions, no fees, no censorship (other than good taste) on what you can display inside your own business.

Celebrate your success and the success of your students by acknowledging their achievements in displays, flyers, posters, news clippings, etc.

Continually add new material to keep things current so that visitors are always seeing something different and current so that they don't become blinded by repetition.

Make it something that your staff and students can contribute to. This will make everyone feel more included and it will lessen your work load as others supply you with fresh content and they will be extremely proud to see their contributions on display, being acknowledged by you and others.

Quick Image Guide For Branding Online

You have a Logo/Brand Image so put it everywhere...
Have your logo saved in the following sizes to be used in your online marketing with social media and emails

Facebook
Website
Google Places
Photos

Twitter
LinkedIn
Emails

Facebook
Cover Image – 851x315 pixels
Profile Image – 160x160 pixels
Post Photo – 404x404 pixels

Twitter
Profile Image – 73x73 pixels (overall 80x80)
Header Image – 520x260 pixels

Your Own Website
This varies as you generally have a lot of freedom to make it any size you want.

LinkedIn Company Page
Profile Image – 100x60 pixels
Overview Cover Image – 646x220 pixels
Career Cover Image – 974x238 pixels
Product/Services Image – 646x220 pixels
Product Thumnail – 100x80 pixels

Google Places
Google allows you to add 6 photos on your Business Listing, make sure that one of your images is a good quality image of your Logo, also have a photo of the outside of your building with the external signage visable.

Emails
Most email services (outlook, gmail, yahoo, etc) allow you to build a personalised signature. Add a small image of your logo into this signature so that everytime you send an email the recpiant is seeing your brand.

Photos
Get your Brand Image saved as a .png file with a clear background that you can use to add over the top of any photos you are posting.

This is a great viral marketing technique for Facebook. Place your Logo on the corner of every photo before you post it and then tag the people in the photo. The photo will appear on their timeline where their friends and family can see it...

People you've never met will be looking at, liking and commenting on the photo because their friend/cousin/grandchild is in it. Everyone that sees it will also see your logo.

Having photos of happy students being shared around on social media with your logo on them is great free publicity

Note: Your student enrollment contract should have a waiver allowing you to post photos of your students

Attractive Vs Powerful Business Cards

Anyone that owns a Business should have and always carry Business Cards...

...But most Business Cards are Crap...

Business Cards Should <u>Not</u> Focus Completely On Branding!

When it comes to business card design, the majority of cards look the same and they fail to do what a business card is supposed to do.

A Business Card's sole purpose is to advertise what your business is and why they should contact you.

The message must be simple, loud and clear to everybody that sees it.

<u>**Most Business Cards FAIL At This!**</u>

Most business cards have the name of the company, the persons name and their contact details... and that's it! Maybe they have a slogan or a logo or a pretty picture but they lack the elements that attract customers.

Here are my very serious guidelines for a successful Business Card Design...

- **A Picture of You**
- Add An Offer/Call To Action
- **Testimonials**
- A Guarantee (Risk Reversal)
- **Contact Details**
- Website URL
- **Quality Production**

I'll run through these elements in more detail.

A Picture of You - This should be a head shot showing the top of your chest and shoulders. Wearing a suit or your Instructors uniform. Be relaxed and happy in the photo. Don't be all serious, boring or aggressive... especially if you're trying to attract kids into your school.

Don't use an image of you breaking boards or performing a massive flying kick as these types of pictures will intimidate people and keep them away from your school. You can always show them that stuff later on when they are students.

Add An Offer/Call To Action - Have an offer as the Headline of your card. It goes at the top in large, bold visable text, I suggest Red lettering to grab attention and make it stand out.

The offer is up to you but it has to grab their

interest straight away and give them a reason to contact you. Just think about what's in it for them, why should they call you and not some other Martial Arts School?.
Here are some examples...

"<u>30 Day</u> FREE Trial"
Or
"FREE Uniform and <u>Private Lesson</u>"

Testimonials - Get your students (or the parents) to write you a testimonial. Now pick out the best and put it on your Business Card along with their name.

You want a testimonial that addresses a possible problem and explains how your school rises above it and how great it is, eg.

"I was worried about my child getting hurt but Fred's MMA Tigers provides safe training and has boosted their confidence and pride."
- Mary Jones

A Guarantee - Risk reversal means you put all the risk on yourself, this way the prospective new students have nothing to lose and hence no reason to fear taking you up on your offer.

Contact Details - All of your contact details including your schools address, phone, fax, website, facebook fanpage, Linkedin profile, youtube channel, etc...
Whatever you have that tells them who you are

you can add onto your business card.
NOTE: <u>Triple check</u> all details are current and accurate before sending to the printers.

Website URL - Make sure your website URL is in bold clear lettering because your website should be one of your best representations of why someone should come to your school (other than a referral from a friend).

Think of your business card as an Ad and it's purpose is to attract new clients into your school... Your website is also an Ad to do the same thing but it holds a lot more info than a business card so make sure it's on your cards for curious people to find and research more about you.

Quality - Don't pinch pennies on your business card printing. Great quality printing is not very expensive these days so there are no excuses.

Find a good quality printer and follow these tips:

- **Choose a thick smooth card**
- Use color to make your Offer and website details stand out.
- **Your Picture should be in color**
- Simple White Background (Don't get too fancy as it will only distract people)

Now that you have great Attractive Business Cards (ones that actually attract new students to your school) you have to be smart about how you hand them out. This is step two of how to get the

best out of your new cards...
Don't just hand them out to everyone you meet or even worse give them to your students or junior staff to hand out to a crowd. That's almost as bad as email spamming and 99% of your cards will end up in the trash.

Here are some guidelines for **when** you can **Hand Them Out:**

- After you have had a conversation with someone about martial arts and you judge them to be a prospective new student.
- **After you have invited them to your school**
- After you've made it clear what you do and what you can do for them or their children.
- **Ask for their details first before providing them with your details.**

This may sound like you won't be handing out many cards but that all depends on you and how many people you meet and talk with.

If you meet someone, have a great conversation and find out what they like, what they want and they seem interested in you and your school before giving them your card then you have a very high chance of them coming in to take you up on your offer.

Follow these details and you will hand out less cards but get a much better response.

Your Branding Tracker Checklist

Write in the Start Date and Completion Date for each ittem on the checklist.

Branding	Started	Completed
Brand Image/Logo Creation		
Club Uniforms		
Casual Tees		
Caps		
Training Bags		
Jacket/Hoodie		
Comapny Car Signage		
Comapny Car Signage		
Car/Bumper Stickers		
External Signage		
Internal Signage		
Online Branding - Facebook		
Online Branding - Twitter		
Online Branding – LinkedIn		
Online Branding – Google Places/ Business Listing		

Note: The Logo/Brand Creation is the first step, after that you can do the rest in any order you choose. I suggest you start with the casual t-shirts as these produce quick profits which you can then reinvest into your signage and marketing.

Thank You

I write these books for you more than me as I hope that I can help you grow your business while having fun and making a more profit.

I really appreciate your feedback and love hearing about the successes you have with your students and your business. Please contact me anytime via my personal website listed below if you have any questions or if there are any topics you would like me to cover in a futre book.

Train Hard, Live Well

Cheers

AJ Perry

Ps. Please take a minute to leave a review on Amazon for others to know if this book is helpful.

To further support this author, please post a review on Amazon after you finish reading this book.

For all books writen by Aaron J. Perry go to
Amazon's Aaron J. Perry Page

To find out when A.J.Perry has new books available and to see what else he is currently working on visit his personal website and join his free updates group...
www.aaronjperry.com

Acknowledgements

I would like to thank the Inner Circle Members of the Martial Games Newsletter for sharing your successs stories with me over the years.

Seeing your Martial Arts Schools grow while others have unfortunately disappeared due to the recent economic tough times has been inspiring.

Treating your business and marketing with the same consistant attention that you pay to your Martial Art has brought it's own rewards.

The friendly sharing of your ideas, methods, tricks, tips and results has helped all involved in the journey so far and I look forward to continuing to learn, teach and grow with you all.

I would also like to thank all of the people I have trained with over the years that have helped me become a well rounded fighter and person. I always try to improve but the more I learn the more I realize I don't know, and I now know for certain that there are always people bigger, tougher, smarter, faster and more talented than me which keeps my ego in check. It's an honour to have met and trained with you...

Resources

Royalty Free Images

123RF is the cheapest place I've found with a great selection of photos, vector art, animations and audio
http://www.123rf.com

Graphic Designers

You can find designers on Fiverr for $5-$20
http://fiverr.com/

99 Designs gets designers to compete to create your new logo/brand and only pay for the one you choose as the winner. Great way to get a lot of ideas if you don't know what you want
http://99designs.com/

Tees and More

Teespring is great for quick orders releasing new designs to your students/friends.
http://teespring.com/

CafePress allows you to put your Logo/Brand onto a wide range of products and build an online store for continuous sales but their pricing is higher so your profit is lower. Still it's a helpful option for extending your Brand
http://www.cafepress.com

www.ingramcontent.com/pod-product-compliance
Lightning Source LLC
Chambersburg PA
CBHW071809170526
45167CB00003B/1233